MW01114948

THIS WEEKS CONCEPT :: _____

TOPICS OF DISCUSSION :: _____

_____

SYNTHESIS ::

Creating is about putting elements together to form a functional whole, and reorganizing elements into a new pattern or structure by strategic planning or production.

EVALUATE ::

Evaluating involves making judgements based on criteria and standards through checking and critiquing.

ANALYSIS ::

The analyzing process involves breaking down material or concepts into parts determining ow the parts interrelate to one another or to an overall structure or purpose.

APPLICATION ::

Applying refers to situations where learned material is used through products like models, diagrams, presentations, interviews and simulations.

COMPREHENSION ::
UNDERSTANDING ::

Constructing meaning from different types of function be they written or graphic.

KNOWLEDGE ::
VOCABULARY ::

When memory is used to produce, retrieve or recite definitions, facts or lists, one has achieved a knowledge base.

WEEK ____ / ____ :: _____ % COMPLETE.   DATE :: _____

AGE/INSTRUCTIONAL LEVEL :: _____

CREATE

CRITIQUE

RELATE

NEW USES

EXPLAIN

RECALL

3

THIS WEEKS CONCEPT :: _____

TOPICS OF DISCUSSION :: _____

_____

SYNTHESIS ::

Creating is about putting elements together to form a functional whole, and reorganizing elements into a new pattern or structure by strategic planning or production.

EVALUATE ::

Evaluating involves making judgements based on criteria and standards through checking and critiquing.

ANALYSIS ::

The analyzing process involves breaking down material or concepts into parts determining ow the parts interrelate to one another or to an overall structure or purpose.

APPLICATION ::

Applying refers to situations where learned material is used through products like models, diagrams, presentations, interviews and simulations.

COMPREHENSION ::
UNDERSTANDING ::

Constructing meaning from different types of function be they written or graphic.

KNOWLEDGE ::
VOCABULARY ::

When memory is used to produce, retrieve or recite definitions, facts or lists, one has achieved a knowledge base.

WEEK ____ / ____ :: _____ % COMPLETE.   DATE :: _____

AGE/INSTRUCTIONAL LEVEL :: _____

CREATE

CRITIQUE

RELATE

NEW USES

EXPLAIN

RECALL

5

SYNTHESIS ::

Creating is about putting elements together to form a functional whole, and reorganizing elements into a new pattern or structure by strategic planning or production.

EVALUATE ::

Evaluating involves making judgements based on criteria and standards through checking and critiquing.

ANALYSIS ::

The analyzing process involves breaking down material or concepts into parts determining ow the parts interrelate to one another or to an overall structure or purpose.

APPLICATION ::

Applying refers to situations where learned material is used through products like models, diagrams, presentations, interviews and simulations.

COMPREHENSION ::
UNDERSTANDING ::

Constructing meaning from different types of function be they written or graphic.

KNOWLEDGE ::
VOCABULARY ::

When memory is used to produce, retrieve or recite definitions, facts or lists, one has achieved a knowledge base.

WEEK ____ / ____ :: _____ % COMPLETE.   DATE :: _____

AGE/INSTRUCTIONAL LEVEL :: _____

CREATE

CRITIQUE

RELATE

NEW USES

EXPLAIN

RECALL

7

THIS WEEKS CONCEPT :: _____

TOPICS OF DISCUSSION :: _____

_____

SYNTHESIS ::

Creating is about putting elements together to form a functional whole, and reorganizing elements into a new pattern or structure by strategic planning or production.

EVALUATE ::

Evaluating involves making judgements based on criteria and standards through checking and critiquing.

ANALYSIS ::

The analyzing process involves breaking down material or concepts into parts determining ow the parts interrelate to one another or to an overall structure or purpose.

APPLICATION ::

Applying refers to situations where learned material is used through products like models, diagrams, presentations, interviews and simulations.

COMPREHENSION ::
UNDERSTANDING ::

Constructing meaning from different types of function be they written or graphic.

KNOWLEDGE ::
VOCABULARY ::

When memory is used to produce, retrieve or recite definitions, facts or lists, one has achieved a knowledge base.

WEEK ____ / ____ :: ____ % COMPLETE.   DATE :: _____

AGE/INSTRUCTIONAL LEVEL :: _____

CREATE

CRITIQUE

RELATE

NEW USES

EXPLAIN

RECALL

9

THIS WEEKS CONCEPT :: _____

TOPICS OF DISCUSSION :: _____

_____

SYNTHESIS ::
Creating is about putting elements together to form a functional whole, and reorganizing elements into a new pattern or structure by strategic planning or production.

EVALUATE ::
Evaluating involves making judgements based on criteria and standards through checking and critiquing.

ANALYSIS ::
The analyzing process involves breaking down material or concepts into parts determining ow the parts interrelate to one another or to an overall structure or purpose.

APPLICATION ::
Applying refers to situations where learned material is used through products like models, diagrams, presentations, interviews and simulations.

COMPREHENSION ::
UNDERSTANDING ::
Constructing meaning from different types of function be they written or graphic.

KNOWLEDGE ::
VOCABULARY ::
When memory is used to produce, retrieve or recite definitions, facts or lists, one has achieved a knowledge base.

WEEK ____ / ____ :: _____ % COMPLETE.   DATE :: _____

AGE/INSTRUCTIONAL LEVEL :: _____

CREATE

CRITIQUE

RELATE

NEW USES

EXPLAIN

RECALL

11

SYNTHESIS ::

Creating is about putting elements together to form a functional whole, and reorganizing elements into a new pattern or structure by strategic planning or production.

EVALUATE ::

Evaluating involves making judgements based on criteria and standards through checking and critiquing.

ANALYSIS ::

The analyzing process involves breaking down material or concepts into parts determining ow the parts interrelate to one another or to an overall structure or purpose.

APPLICATION ::

Applying refers to situations where learned material is used through products like models, diagrams, presentations, interviews and simulations.

COMPREHENSION ::
UNDERSTANDING ::

Constructing meaning from different types of function be they written or graphic.

KNOWLEDGE ::
VOCABULARY ::

When memory is used to produce, retrieve or recite definitions, facts or lists, one has achieved a knowledge base.

WEEK ____ / ____ :: _____ % COMPLETE.   DATE :: _____

AGE/INSTRUCTIONAL LEVEL :: _____

CREATE

CRITIQUE

RELATE

NEW USES

EXPLAIN

RECALL

13

THIS WEEKS CONCEPT :: _____

TOPICS OF DISCUSSION :: _____

_____

SYNTHESIS ::
Creating is about putting elements together to form a functional whole, and reorganizing elements into a new pattern or structure by strategic planning or production.

EVALUATE ::
Evaluating involves making judgements based on criteria and standards through checking and critiquing.

ANALYSIS ::
The analyzing process involves breaking down material or concepts into parts determining ow the parts interrelate to one another or to an overall structure or purpose.

APPLICATION ::
Applying refers to situations where learned material is used through products like models, diagrams, presentations, interviews and simulations.

COMPREHENSION ::
UNDERSTANDING ::
Constructing meaning from different types of function be they written or graphic.

KNOWLEDGE ::
VOCABULARY ::
When memory is used to produce, retrieve or recite definitions, facts or lists, one has achieved a knowledge base.

CREATE

CRITIQUE

RELATE

NEW USES

EXPLAIN

RECALL

THIS WEEKS CONCEPT :: _____

TOPICS OF DISCUSSION :: _____

_____

SYNTHESIS ::
Creating is about putting elements together to form a functional whole, and reorganizing elements into a new pattern or structure by strategic planning or production.

EVALUATE ::
Evaluating involves making judgements based on criteria and standards through checking and critiquing.

ANALYSIS ::
The analyzing process involves breaking down material or concepts into parts determining ow the parts interrelate to one another or to an overall structure or purpose.

APPLICATION ::
Applying refers to situations where learned material is used through products like models, diagrams, presentations, interviews and simulations.

COMPREHENSION ::
UNDERSTANDING ::
Constructing meaning from different types of function be they written or graphic.

KNOWLEDGE ::
VOCABULARY ::
When memory is used to produce, retrieve or recite definitions, facts or lists, one has achieved a knowledge base.

WEEK ____ /____ :: _____ % COMPLETE.   DATE :: _____

AGE/INSTRUCTIONAL LEVEL :: _____

CREATE

CRITIQUE

RELATE

NEW USES

EXPLAIN

RECALL

THIS WEEKS CONCEPT :: _____

TOPICS OF DISCUSSION :: _____

_____

SYNTHESIS ::

Creating is about putting elements together to form a functional whole, and reorganizing elements into a new pattern or structure by strategic planning or production.

EVALUATE ::

Evaluating involves making judgements based on criteria and standards through checking and critiquing.

ANALYSIS ::

The analyzing process involves breaking down material or concepts into parts determining ow the parts interrelate to one another or to an overall structure or purpose.

APPLICATION ::

Applying refers to situations where learned material is used through products like models, diagrams, presentations, interviews and simulations.

COMPREHENSION ::
UNDERSTANDING ::

Constructing meaning from different types of function be they written or graphic.

KNOWLEDGE ::
VOCABULARY ::

When memory is used to produce, retrieve or recite definitions, facts or lists, one has achieved a knowledge base.

WEEK ____ / ____ :: ____ % COMPLETE.   DATE :: _____

AGE/INSTRUCTIONAL LEVEL :: _____

CREATE

CRITIQUE

RELATE

NEW USES

EXPLAIN

RECALL

19

THIS WEEKS CONCEPT :: _____

TOPICS OF DISCUSSION :: _____

_____

SYNTHESIS ::

Creating is about putting elements together to form a functional whole, and reorganizing elements into a new pattern or structure by strategic planning or production.

EVALUATE ::

Evaluating involves making judgements based on criteria and standards through checking and critiquing.

ANALYSIS ::

The analyzing process involves breaking down material or concepts into parts determining ow the parts interrelate to one another or to an overall structure or purpose.

APPLICATION ::

Applying refers to situations where learned material is used through products like models, diagrams, presentations, interviews and simulations.

COMPREHENSION ::
UNDERSTANDING ::

Constructing meaning from different types of function be they written or graphic.

KNOWLEDGE ::
VOCABULARY ::

When memory is used to produce, retrieve or recite definitions, facts or lists, one has achieved a knowledge base.

WEEK ____ / ____ :: ____ % COMPLETE.   DATE :: _____

AGE/INSTRUCTIONAL LEVEL :: _____

CREATE

CRITIQUE

RELATE

NEW USES

EXPLAIN

RECALL

21

_____

_____

_____

SYNTHESIS ::

Creating is about putting elements together to form a functional whole, and reorganizing elements into a new pattern or structure by strategic planning or production.

EVALUATE ::

Evaluating involves making judgements based on criteria and standards through checking and critiquing.

ANALYSIS ::

The analyzing process involves breaking down material or concepts into parts determining ow the parts interrelate to one another or to an overall structure or purpose.

APPLICATION ::

Applying refers to situations where learned material is used through products like models, diagrams, presentations, interviews and simulations.

COMPREHENSION ::
UNDERSTANDING ::

Constructing meaning from different types of function be they written or graphic.

KNOWLEDGE ::
VOCABULARY ::

When memory is used to produce, retrieve or recite definitions, facts or lists, one has achieved a knowledge base.

WEEK ___ / ___ :: ___ % COMPLETE. DATE :: _____

AGE/INSTRUCTIONAL LEVEL :: _____

CREATE

CRITIQUE

RELATE

NEW USES

EXPLAIN

RECALL

23

THIS WEEKS CONCEPT :: _____

TOPICS OF DISCUSSION :: _____

_____

SYNTHESIS ::

Creating is about putting elements together to form a functional whole, and reorganizing elements into a new pattern or structure by strategic planning or production.

EVALUATE ::

Evaluating involves making judgements based on criteria and standards through checking and critiquing.

ANALYSIS ::

The analyzing process involves breaking down material or concepts into parts determining ow the parts interrelate to one another or to an overall structure or purpose.

APPLICATION ::

Applying refers to situations where learned material is used through products like models, diagrams, presentations, interviews and simulations.

COMPREHENSION ::
UNDERSTANDING ::

Constructing meaning from different types of function be they written or graphic.

KNOWLEDGE ::
VOCABULARY ::

When memory is used to produce, retrieve or recite definitions, facts or lists, one has achieved a knowledge base.

WEEK ____ / ____ :: ____ % COMPLETE.   DATE :: _____

AGE/INSTRUCTIONAL LEVEL :: _____

CREATE

CRITIQUE

RELATE

NEW USES

EXPLAIN

RECALL

THIS WEEKS CONCEPT :: _____

TOPICS OF DISCUSSION :: _____

_____

SYNTHESIS ::
Creating is about putting elements together to form a functional whole, and reorganizing elements into a new pattern or structure by strategic planning or production.

EVALUATE ::
Evaluating involves making judgements based on criteria and standards through checking and critiquing.

ANALYSIS ::
The analyzing process involves breaking down material or concepts into parts determining ow the parts interrelate to one another or to an overall structure or purpose.

APPLICATION ::
Applying refers to situations where learned material is used through products like models, diagrams, presentations, interviews and simulations.

COMPREHENSION ::
UNDERSTANDING ::
Constructing meaning from different types of function be they written or graphic.

KNOWLEDGE ::
VOCABULARY ::
When memory is used to produce, retrieve or recite definitions, facts or lists, one has achieved a knowledge base.

WEEK ____ / ____ :: _____ % COMPLETE.   DATE :: _____

AGE/INSTRUCTIONAL LEVEL :: _____

CREATE

CRITIQUE

RELATE

NEW USES

EXPLAIN

RECALL

27

THIS WEEKS CONCEPT :: _____

TOPICS OF DISCUSSION :: _____

_____

SYNTHESIS ::

Creating is about putting elements together to form a functional whole, and reorganizing elements into a new pattern or structure by strategic planning or production.

EVALUATE ::

Evaluating involves making judgements based on criteria and standards through checking and critiquing.

ANALYSIS ::

The analyzing process involves breaking down material or concepts into parts determining ow the parts interrelate to one another or to an overall structure or purpose.

APPLICATION ::

Applying refers to situations where learned material is used through products like models, diagrams, presentations, interviews and simulations.

COMPREHENSION ::
UNDERSTANDING ::

Constructing meaning from different types of function be they written or graphic.

KNOWLEDGE ::
VOCABULARY ::

When memory is used to produce, retrieve or recite definitions, facts or lists, one has achieved a knowledge base.

WEEK ____ / ____ :: ____ % COMPLETE.   DATE :: _____

AGE/INSTRUCTIONAL LEVEL :: _____

CREATE

CRITIQUE

RELATE

NEW USES

EXPLAIN

RECALL

29

THIS WEEKS CONCEPT :: _____

TOPICS OF DISCUSSION :: _____

_____

SYNTHESIS ::

Creating is about putting elements together to form a functional whole, and reorganizing elements into a new pattern or structure by strategic planning or production.

EVALUATE ::

Evaluating involves making judgements based on criteria and standards through checking and critiquing.

ANALYSIS ::

The analyzing process involves breaking down material or concepts into parts determining ow the parts interrelate to one another or to an overall structure or purpose.

APPLICATION ::

Applying refers to situations where learned material is used through products like models, diagrams, presentations, interviews and simulations.

COMPREHENSION ::
UNDERSTANDING ::

Constructing meaning from different types of function be they written or graphic.

KNOWLEDGE ::
VOCABULARY ::

When memory is used to produce, retrieve or recite definitions, facts or lists, one has achieved a knowledge base.

CREATE

CRITIQUE

RELATE

NEW USES

EXPLAIN

RECALL

THIS WEEKS CONCEPT :: _____

TOPICS OF DISCUSSION :: _____

_____

SYNTHESIS ::
Creating is about putting elements together to form a functional whole, and reorganizing elements into a new pattern or structure by strategic planning or production.

EVALUATE ::
Evaluating involves making judgements based on criteria and standards through checking and critiquing.

ANALYSIS ::
The analyzing process involves breaking down material or concepts into parts determining ow the parts interrelate to one another or to an overall structure or purpose.

APPLICATION ::
Applying refers to situations where learned material is used through products like models, diagrams, presentations, interviews and simulations.

COMPREHENSION ::
UNDERSTANDING ::
Constructing meaning from different types of function be they written or graphic.

KNOWLEDGE ::
VOCABULARY ::
When memory is used to produce, retrieve or recite definitions, facts or lists, one has achieved a knowledge base.

WEEK ___ / ___ :: ___ % COMPLETE.   DATE :: _____

AGE/INSTRUCTIONAL LEVEL :: _____

CREATE

CRITIQUE

RELATE

NEW USES

EXPLAIN

RECALL

33

THIS WEEKS CONCEPT :: _____

TOPICS OF DISCUSSION :: _____

_____

SYNTHESIS ::
Creating is about putting elements together to form a functional whole, and reorganizing elements into a new pattern or structure by strategic planning or production.

EVALUATE ::
Evaluating involves making judgements based on criteria and standards through checking and critiquing.

ANALYSIS ::
The analyzing process involves breaking down material or concepts into parts determining ow the parts interrelate to one another or to an overall structure or purpose.

APPLICATION ::
Applying refers to situations where learned material is used through products like models, diagrams, presentations, interviews and simulations.

COMPREHENSION ::
UNDERSTANDING ::
Constructing meaning from different types of function be they written or graphic.

KNOWLEDGE ::
VOCABULARY ::
When memory is used to produce, retrieve or recite definitions, facts or lists, one has achieved a knowledge base.

WEEK _____ /_____ :: _____ % COMPLETE.   DATE :: _____

AGE/INSTRUCTIONAL LEVEL :: _____

CREATE

CRITIQUE

RELATE

NEW USES

EXPLAIN

RECALL

THIS WEEKS CONCEPT :: _____

TOPICS OF DISCUSSION :: _____

_____

SYNTHESIS ::

Creating is about putting elements together to form a functional whole, and reorganizing elements into a new pattern or structure by strategic planning or production.

EVALUATE ::

Evaluating involves making judgements based on criteria and standards through checking and critiquing.

ANALYSIS ::

The analyzing process involves breaking down material or concepts into parts determining ow the parts interrelate to one another or to an overall structure or purpose.

APPLICATION ::

Applying refers to situations where learned material is used through products like models, diagrams, presentations, interviews and simulations.

COMPREHENSION ::
UNDERSTANDING ::

Constructing meaning from different types of function be they written or graphic.

KNOWLEDGE ::
VOCABULARY ::

When memory is used to produce, retrieve or recite definitions, facts or lists, one has achieved a knowledge base.

WEEK ____/____ :: _____ % COMPLETE.   DATE :: _____

AGE/INSTRUCTIONAL LEVEL :: _____

CREATE

CRITIQUE

RELATE

NEW USES

EXPLAIN

RECALL

THIS WEEKS CONCEPT :: _____

TOPICS OF DISCUSSION :: _____

_____

SYNTHESIS ::

Creating is about putting elements together to form a functional whole, and reorganizing elements into a new pattern or structure by strategic planning or production.

EVALUATE ::

Evaluating involves making judgements based on criteria and standards through checking and critiquing.

ANALYSIS ::

The analyzing process involves breaking down material or concepts into parts determining ow the parts interrelate to one another or to an overall structure or purpose.

APPLICATION ::

Applying refers to situations where learned material is used through products like models, diagrams, presentations, interviews and simulations.

COMPREHENSION ::
UNDERSTANDING ::

Constructing meaning from different types of function be they written or graphic.

KNOWLEDGE ::
VOCABULARY ::

When memory is used to produce, retrieve or recite definitions, facts or lists, one has achieved a knowledge base.

WEEK ___ / ___ :: ___ % COMPLETE. DATE :: _____

AGE/INSTRUCTIONAL LEVEL :: _____

CREATE

CRITIQUE

RELATE

NEW USES

EXPLAIN

RECALL

THIS WEEKS CONCEPT :: _____

TOPICS OF DISCUSSION :: _____

_____

SYNTHESIS ::

Creating is about putting elements together to form a functional whole, and reorganizing elements into a new pattern or structure by strategic planning or production.

EVALUATE ::

Evaluating involves making judgements based on criteria and standards through checking and critiquing.

ANALYSIS ::

The analyzing process involves breaking down material or concepts into parts determining ow the parts interrelate to one another or to an overall structure or purpose.

APPLICATION ::

Applying refers to situations where learned material is used through products like models, diagrams, presentations, interviews and simulations.

COMPREHENSION ::
UNDERSTANDING ::

Constructing meaning from different types of function be they written or graphic.

KNOWLEDGE ::
VOCABULARY ::

When memory is used to produce, retrieve or recite definitions, facts or lists, one has achieved a knowledge base.

WEEK ____ / ____ :: _____ % COMPLETE.   DATE :: _____

AGE/INSTRUCTIONAL LEVEL :: _____

CREATE

CRITIQUE

RELATE

NEW USES

EXPLAIN

RECALL

41

THIS WEEKS CONCEPT :: _____

TOPICS OF DISCUSSION :: _____

_____

SYNTHESIS ::

Creating is about putting elements together to form a functional whole, and reorganizing elements into a new pattern or structure by strategic planning or production.

EVALUATE ::

Evaluating involves making judgements based on criteria and standards through checking and critiquing.

ANALYSIS ::

The analyzing process involves breaking down material or concepts into parts determining ow the parts interrelate to one another or to an overall structure or purpose.

APPLICATION ::

Applying refers to situations where learned material is used through products like models, diagrams, presentations, interviews and simulations.

COMPREHENSION ::
UNDERSTANDING ::

Constructing meaning from different types of function be they written or graphic.

KNOWLEDGE ::
VOCABULARY ::

When memory is used to produce, retrieve or recite definitions, facts or lists, one has achieved a knowledge base.

WEEK ____ / ____ :: _____ % COMPLETE.   DATE :: _____

AGE/INSTRUCTIONAL LEVEL :: _____

CREATE

CRITIQUE

RELATE

NEW USES

EXPLAIN

RECALL

TOPICS OF DISCUSSION :: _____

_____

SYNTHESIS ::

Creating is about putting elements together to form a functional whole, and reorganizing elements into a new pattern or structure by strategic planning or production.

EVALUATE ::

Evaluating involves making judgements based on criteria and standards through checking and critiquing.

ANALYSIS ::

The analyzing process involves breaking down material or concepts into parts determining ow the parts interrelate to one another or to an overall structure or purpose.

APPLICATION ::

Applying refers to situations where learned material is used through products like models, diagrams, presentations, interviews and simulations.

COMPREHENSION ::
UNDERSTANDING ::

Constructing meaning from different types of function be they written or graphic.

KNOWLEDGE ::
VOCABULARY ::

When memory is used to produce, retrieve or recite definitions, facts or lists, one has achieved a knowledge base.

WEEK ____ / ____ :: ____ % COMPLETE. DATE :: _____

AGE/INSTRUCTIONAL LEVEL :: _____

CREATE

CRITIQUE

RELATE

NEW USES

EXPLAIN

RECALL

THIS WEEKS CONCEPT :: _____

TOPICS OF DISCUSSION :: _____

_____

SYNTHESIS ::

Creating is about putting elements together to form a functional whole, and reorganizing elements into a new pattern or structure by strategic planning or production.

EVALUATE ::

Evaluating involves making judgements based on criteria and standards through checking and critiquing.

ANALYSIS ::

The analyzing process involves breaking down material or concepts into parts determining ow the parts interrelate to one another or to an overall structure or purpose.

APPLICATION ::

Applying refers to situations where learned material is used through products like models, diagrams, presentations, interviews and simulations.

COMPREHENSION ::
UNDERSTANDING ::

Constructing meaning from different types of function be they written or graphic.

KNOWLEDGE ::
VOCABULARY ::

When memory is used to produce, retrieve or recite definitions, facts or lists, one has achieved a knowledge base.

WEEK ____ / ____ :: ____ % COMPLETE. DATE :: _____

AGE/INSTRUCTIONAL LEVEL :: _____

CREATE

CRITIQUE

RELATE

NEW USES

EXPLAIN

RECALL

47

THIS WEEKS CONCEPT :: _____

TOPICS OF DISCUSSION :: _____

_____

SYNTHESIS ::

Creating is about putting elements together to form a functional whole, and reorganizing elements into a new pattern or structure by strategic planning or production.

EVALUATE ::

Evaluating involves making judgements based on criteria and standards through checking and critiquing.

ANALYSIS ::

The analyzing process involves breaking down material or concepts into parts determining ow the parts interrelate to one another or to an overall structure or purpose.

APPLICATION ::

Applying refers to situations where learned material is used through products like models, diagrams, presentations, interviews and simulations.

COMPREHENSION ::
UNDERSTANDING ::

Constructing meaning from different types of function be they written or graphic.

KNOWLEDGE ::
VOCABULARY ::

When memory is used to produce, retrieve or recite definitions, facts or lists, one has achieved a knowledge base.

CREATE

CRITIQUE

RELATE

NEW USES

EXPLAIN

RECALL

THIS WEEKS CONCEPT :: _____

TOPICS OF DISCUSSION :: _____

_____

SYNTHESIS ::

Creating is about putting elements together to form a functional whole, and reorganizing elements into a new pattern or structure by strategic planning or production.

EVALUATE ::

Evaluating involves making judgements based on criteria and standards through checking and critiquing.

ANALYSIS ::

The analyzing process involves breaking down material or concepts into parts determining ow the parts interrelate to one another or to an overall structure or purpose.

APPLICATION ::

Applying refers to situations where learned material is used through products like models, diagrams, presentations, interviews and simulations.

COMPREHENSION ::
UNDERSTANDING ::

Constructing meaning from different types of function be they written or graphic.

KNOWLEDGE ::
VOCABULARY ::

When memory is used to produce, retrieve or recite definitions, facts or lists, one has achieved a knowledge base.

WEEK ____ /____ :: _____ % COMPLETE.   DATE :: _____

AGE/INSTRUCTIONAL LEVEL :: _____

CREATE

CRITIQUE

RELATE

NEW USES

EXPLAIN

RECALL

THIS WEEKS CONCEPT :: _____

TOPICS OF DISCUSSION :: _____

_____

SYNTHESIS ::

Creating is about putting elements together to form a functional whole, and reorganizing elements into a new pattern or structure by strategic planning or production.

EVALUATE ::

Evaluating involves making judgements based on criteria and standards through checking and critiquing.

ANALYSIS ::

The analyzing process involves breaking down material or concepts into parts determining ow the parts interrelate to one another or to an overall structure or purpose.

APPLICATION ::

Applying refers to situations where learned material is used through products like models, diagrams, presentations, interviews and simulations.

COMPREHENSION ::
UNDERSTANDING ::

Constructing meaning from different types of function be they written or graphic.

KNOWLEDGE ::
VOCABULARY ::

When memory is used to produce, retrieve or recite definitions, facts or lists, one has achieved a knowledge base.

WEEK ____ / ____ :: _____ % COMPLETE.   DATE :: _____

AGE/INSTRUCTIONAL LEVEL :: _____

CREATE

CRITIQUE

RELATE

NEW USES

EXPLAIN

RECALL

53

THIS WEEKS CONCEPT :: _____

TOPICS OF DISCUSSION :: _____

_____

SYNTHESIS ::

Creating is about putting elements together to form a functional whole, and reorganizing elements into a new pattern or structure by strategic planning or production.

EVALUATE ::

Evaluating involves making judgements based on criteria and standards through checking and critiquing.

ANALYSIS ::

The analyzing process involves breaking down material or concepts into parts determining ow the parts interrelate to one another or to an overall structure or purpose.

APPLICATION ::

Applying refers to situations where learned material is used through products like models, diagrams, presentations, interviews and simulations.

COMPREHENSION ::
UNDERSTANDING ::

Constructing meaning from different types of function be they written or graphic.

KNOWLEDGE ::
VOCABULARY ::

When memory is used to produce, retrieve or recite definitions, facts or lists, one has achieved a knowledge base.

WEEK ____ / ____ :: _____ % COMPLETE.   DATE :: _____

AGE/INSTRUCTIONAL LEVEL :: _____

CREATE

CRITIQUE

RELATE

NEW USES

EXPLAIN

RECALL

THIS WEEKS CONCEPT :: _____

TOPICS OF DISCUSSION :: _____

_____

SYNTHESIS ::
Creating is about putting elements together to form a functional whole, and reorganizing elements into a new pattern or structure by strategic planning or production.

EVALUATE ::
Evaluating involves making judgements based on criteria and standards through checking and critiquing.

ANALYSIS ::
The analyzing process involves breaking down material or concepts into parts determining ow the parts interrelate to one another or to an overall structure or purpose.

APPLICATION ::
Applying refers to situations where learned material is used through products like models, diagrams, presentations, interviews and simulations.

COMPREHENSION ::
UNDERSTANDING ::
Constructing meaning from different types of function be they written or graphic.

KNOWLEDGE ::
VOCABULARY ::
When memory is used to produce, retrieve or recite definitions, facts or lists, one has achieved a knowledge base.

WEEK ____ /____ :: ____ % COMPLETE.   DATE :: _____

AGE/INSTRUCTIONAL LEVEL :: _____

CREATE

CRITIQUE

RELATE

NEW USES

EXPLAIN

RECALL

THIS WEEKS CONCEPT :: _____

TOPICS OF DISCUSSION :: _____

_____

SYNTHESIS ::
Creating is about putting elements together to form a functional whole, and reorganizing elements into a new pattern or structure by strategic planning or production.

EVALUATE ::
Evaluating involves making judgements based on criteria and standards through checking and critiquing.

ANALYSIS ::
The analyzing process involves breaking down material or concepts into parts determining ow the parts interrelate to one another or to an overall structure or purpose.

APPLICATION ::
Applying refers to situations where learned material is used through products like models, diagrams, presentations, interviews and simulations.

COMPREHENSION ::
UNDERSTANDING ::
Constructing meaning from different types of function be they written or graphic.

KNOWLEDGE ::
VOCABULARY ::
When memory is used to produce, retrieve or recite definitions, facts or lists, one has achieved a knowledge base.

WEEK ____ / ____ :: ____ % COMPLETE. DATE :: _____

AGE/INSTRUCTIONAL LEVEL :: _____

CREATE

CRITIQUE

RELATE

NEW USES

EXPLAIN

RECALL

THIS WEEKS CONCEPT :: _____

TOPICS OF DISCUSSION :: _____

_____

SYNTHESIS ::

Creating is about putting elements together to form a functional whole, and reorganizing elements into a new pattern or structure by strategic planning or production.

EVALUATE ::

Evaluating involves making judgements based on criteria and standards through checking and critiquing.

ANALYSIS ::

The analyzing process involves breaking down material or concepts into parts determining ow the parts interrelate to one another or to an overall structure or purpose.

APPLICATION ::

Applying refers to situations where learned material is used through products like models, diagrams, presentations, interviews and simulations.

COMPREHENSION ::
UNDERSTANDING ::

Constructing meaning from different types of function be they written or graphic.

KNOWLEDGE ::
VOCABULARY ::

When memory is used to produce, retrieve or recite definitions, facts or lists, one has achieved a knowledge base.

WEEK ____ / ____ :: ____ % COMPLETE.   DATE :: _____

AGE/INSTRUCTIONAL LEVEL :: _____

CREATE

CRITIQUE

RELATE

NEW USES

EXPLAIN

RECALL

TOPICS OF DISCUSSION ::

SYNTHESIS ::

Creating is about putting elements together to form a functional whole, and reorganizing elements into a new pattern or structure by strategic planning or production.

EVALUATE ::

Evaluating involves making judgements based on criteria and standards through checking and critiquing.

ANALYSIS ::

The analyzing process involves breaking down material or concepts into parts determining ow the parts interrelate to one another or to an overall structure or purpose.

APPLICATION ::

Applying refers to situations where learned material is used through products like models, diagrams, presentations, interviews and simulations.

COMPREHENSION ::
UNDERSTANDING ::

Constructing meaning from different types of function be they written or graphic.

KNOWLEDGE ::
VOCABULARY ::

When memory is used to produce, retrieve or recite definitions, facts or lists, one has achieved a knowledge base.

CREATE

CRITIQUE

RELATE

NEW USES

EXPLAIN

RECALL

THIS WEEKS CONCEPT :: _____

TOPICS OF DISCUSSION :: _____

_____

SYNTHESIS ::

Creating is about putting elements together to form a functional whole, and reorganizing elements into a new pattern or structure by strategic planning or production.

EVALUATE ::

Evaluating involves making judgements based on criteria and standards through checking and critiquing.

ANALYSIS ::

The analyzing process involves breaking down material or concepts into parts determining ow the parts interrelate to one another or to an overall structure or purpose.

APPLICATION ::

Applying refers to situations where learned material is used through products like models, diagrams, presentations, interviews and simulations.

COMPREHENSION ::
UNDERSTANDING ::

Constructing meaning from different types of function be they written or graphic.

KNOWLEDGE ::
VOCABULARY ::

When memory is used to produce, retrieve or recite definitions, facts or lists, one has achieved a knowledge base.

WEEK _____ / _____ :: _____ % COMPLETE.   DATE :: _____

AGE/INSTRUCTIONAL LEVEL :: _____

CREATE

CRITIQUE

RELATE

NEW USES

EXPLAIN

RECALL

THIS WEEKS CONCEPT :: _____

TOPICS OF DISCUSSION :: _____

_____

SYNTHESIS ::

Creating is about putting elements together to form a functional whole, and reorganizing elements into a new pattern or structure by strategic planning or production.

EVALUATE ::

Evaluating involves making judgements based on criteria and standards through checking and critiquing.

ANALYSIS ::

The analyzing process involves breaking down material or concepts into parts determining ow the parts interrelate to one another or to an overall structure or purpose.

APPLICATION ::

Applying refers to situations where learned material is used through products like models, diagrams, presentations, interviews and simulations.

COMPREHENSION ::
UNDERSTANDING ::

Constructing meaning from different types of function be they written or graphic.

KNOWLEDGE ::
VOCABULARY ::

When memory is used to produce, retrieve or recite definitions, facts or lists, one has achieved a knowledge base.

WEEK ____ /____ :: _____ % COMPLETE.   DATE :: _____

AGE/INSTRUCTIONAL LEVEL :: _____

CREATE

CRITIQUE

RELATE

NEW USES

EXPLAIN

RECALL

67

THIS WEEKS CONCEPT :: _____

TOPICS OF DISCUSSION :: _____

_____

SYNTHESIS ::

Creating is about putting elements together to form a functional whole, and reorganizing elements into a new pattern or structure by strategic planning or production.

EVALUATE ::

Evaluating involves making judgements based on criteria and standards through checking and critiquing.

ANALYSIS ::

The analyzing process involves breaking down material or concepts into parts determining ow the parts interrelate to one another or to an overall structure or purpose.

APPLICATION ::

Applying refers to situations where learned material is used through products like models, diagrams, presentations, interviews and simulations.

COMPREHENSION ::
UNDERSTANDING ::

Constructing meaning from different types of function be they written or graphic.

KNOWLEDGE ::
VOCABULARY ::

When memory is used to produce, retrieve or recite definitions, facts or lists, one has achieved a knowledge base.

WEEK ____ / ____ :: ____ % COMPLETE.   DATE :: _____

AGE/INSTRUCTIONAL LEVEL :: _____

CREATE

CRITIQUE

RELATE

NEW USES

EXPLAIN

RECALL

69

THIS WEEKS CONCEPT :: _____

TOPICS OF DISCUSSION :: _____

_____

SYNTHESIS ::
Creating is about putting elements together to form a functional whole, and reorganizing elements into a new pattern or structure by strategic planning or production.

EVALUATE ::
Evaluating involves making judgements based on criteria and standards through checking and critiquing.

ANALYSIS ::
The analyzing process involves breaking down material or concepts into parts determining ow the parts interrelate to one another or to an overall structure or purpose.

APPLICATION ::
Applying refers to situations where learned material is used through products like models, diagrams, presentations, interviews and simulations.

COMPREHENSION ::
UNDERSTANDING ::
Constructing meaning from different types of function be they written or graphic.

KNOWLEDGE ::
VOCABULARY ::
When memory is used to produce, retrieve or recite definitions, facts or lists, one has achieved a knowledge base.

WEEK ____ / ____ :: ____ % COMPLETE.   DATE :: _____

AGE/INSTRUCTIONAL LEVEL :: _____

CREATE

CRITIQUE

RELATE

NEW USES

EXPLAIN

RECALL

71

THIS WEEKS CONCEPT :: _____

TOPICS OF DISCUSSION :: _____

_____

SYNTHESIS ::
Creating is about putting elements together to form a functional whole, and reorganizing elements into a new pattern or structure by strategic planning or production.

EVALUATE ::
Evaluating involves making judgements based on criteria and standards through checking and critiquing.

ANALYSIS ::
The analyzing process involves breaking down material or concepts into parts determining ow the parts interrelate to one another or to an overall structure or purpose.

APPLICATION ::
Applying refers to situations where learned material is used through products like models, diagrams, presentations, interviews and simulations.

COMPREHENSION ::
UNDERSTANDING ::

Constructing meaning from different types of function be they written or graphic.

KNOWLEDGE ::
VOCABULARY ::

When memory is used to produce, retrieve or recite definitions, facts or lists, one has achieved a knowledge base.

WEEK ____ / ____ :: ____ % COMPLETE.   DATE :: _____

AGE/INSTRUCTIONAL LEVEL :: _____

CREATE

CRITIQUE

RELATE

NEW USES

EXPLAIN

RECALL

73

THIS WEEKS CONCEPT :: _____

TOPICS OF DISCUSSION :: _____

_____

SYNTHESIS ::

Creating is about putting elements together to form a functional whole, and reorganizing elements into a new pattern or structure by strategic planning or production.

EVALUATE ::

Evaluating involves making judgements based on criteria and standards through checking and critiquing.

ANALYSIS ::

The analyzing process involves breaking down material or concepts into parts determining ow the parts interrelate to one another or to an overall structure or purpose.

APPLICATION ::

Applying refers to situations where learned material is used through products like models, diagrams, presentations, interviews and simulations.

COMPREHENSION ::
UNDERSTANDING ::

Constructing meaning from different types of function be they written or graphic.

KNOWLEDGE ::
VOCABULARY ::

When memory is used to produce, retrieve or recite definitions, facts or lists, one has achieved a knowledge base.

WEEK ____ /___ :: ____ % COMPLETE.   DATE :: _____

AGE/INSTRUCTIONAL LEVEL :: _____

CREATE

CRITIQUE

RELATE

NEW USES

EXPLAIN

RECALL

75

THIS WEEKS CONCEPT :: _____

TOPICS OF DISCUSSION :: _____

_____

SYNTHESIS ::

Creating is about putting elements together to form a functional whole, and reorganizing elements into a new pattern or structure by strategic planning or production.

EVALUATE ::

Evaluating involves making judgements based on criteria and standards through checking and critiquing.

ANALYSIS ::

The analyzing process involves breaking down material or concepts into parts determining ow the parts interrelate to one another or to an overall structure or purpose.

APPLICATION ::

Applying refers to situations where learned material is used through products like models, diagrams, presentations, interviews and simulations.

COMPREHENSION ::
UNDERSTANDING ::

Constructing meaning from different types of function be they written or graphic.

KNOWLEDGE ::
VOCABULARY ::

When memory is used to produce, retrieve or recite definitions, facts or lists, one has achieved a knowledge base.

WEEK ____ / ____ :: ____ % COMPLETE.   DATE :: _____

AGE/INSTRUCTIONAL LEVEL :: _____

CREATE

CRITIQUE

RELATE

NEW USES

EXPLAIN

RECALL

77

THIS WEEKS CONCEPT :: _____

TOPICS OF DISCUSSION :: _____

_____

SYNTHESIS ::
Creating is about putting elements together to form a functional whole, and reorganizing elements into a new pattern or structure by strategic planning or production.

EVALUATE ::
Evaluating involves making judgements based on criteria and standards through checking and critiquing.

ANALYSIS ::
The analyzing process involves breaking down material or concepts into parts determining ow the parts interrelate to one another or to an overall structure or purpose.

APPLICATION ::
Applying refers to situations where learned material is used through products like models, diagrams, presentations, interviews and simulations.

COMPREHENSION ::
UNDERSTANDING ::
Constructing meaning from different types of function be they written or graphic.

KNOWLEDGE ::
VOCABULARY ::
When memory is used to produce, retrieve or recite definitions, facts or lists, one has achieved a knowledge base.

WEEK ____ /___ :: ____ % COMPLETE.   DATE :: _____

AGE/INSTRUCTIONAL LEVEL :: _____

CREATE

CRITIQUE

RELATE

NEW USES

EXPLAIN

RECALL

TOPICS OF DISCUSSION :: _____
_____

SYNTHESIS ::

Creating is about putting elements together to form a functional whole, and reorganizing elements into a new pattern or structure by strategic planning or production.

EVALUATE ::

Evaluating involves making judgements based on criteria and standards through checking and critiquing.

ANALYSIS ::

The analyzing process involves breaking down material or concepts into parts determining ow the parts interrelate to one another or to an overall structure or purpose.

APPLICATION ::

Applying refers to situations where learned material is used through products like models, diagrams, presentations, interviews and simulations.

COMPREHENSION ::
UNDERSTANDING ::

Constructing meaning from different types of function be they written or graphic.

KNOWLEDGE ::
VOCABULARY ::

When memory is used to produce, retrieve or recite definitions, facts or lists, one has achieved a knowledge base.

WEEK ___/___ :: ___% COMPLETE. DATE :: _____

AGE/INSTRUCTIONAL LEVEL :: _____

CREATE

CRITIQUE

RELATE

NEW USES

EXPLAIN

RECALL

Made in the USA
Monee, IL
27 October 2020